DEDICATION PAGE

ISBN-13:
978-1974376254

ISBN-10:
1974376257

ME:

This book is fondly dedicated to my father, the late Ernest Hayward, one of the most disciplined and determined people I have ever met. Also my Mother, one of the most creative people I ever met.

YOU:

This is your Instruction book, your How-To get it done. Written simple for parent and children instruction. This is your Fun!!!!! Save each One You Complete and Collect them. This is for you, GET UP GET GOING, MAKE MONEY AND CREATE!!!!!!!

Ohh and reading, writing, Art, and thinking is a good Thing, just look at what our heavenly father said about it in his word.

Isaiah 64:8 ESV

But now, O Lord, you are our Father; we are the clay, and you are our potter; we are all the work of your hand.

Exodus 35:35 ESV

He has filled them with skill to do every sort of work done by an engraver or by a designer or by an embroiderer in blue and purple and scarlet yarns and fine twined linen, or by a weaver—by any sort of workman or skilled designer.

Habakkuk 2:2King James Version (KJV)

2 And the Lord answered me, and said, Write the vision, and make it plain upon tables, that he may run that readeth it.

US:

At The end of this Book is a space for Comments, thoughts and Concerns. Use this space to write down your goals.

WRITE IT DOWN – Goals that are not in writing are not goals at all and could end up as discarded wishes. When you write it down, you take it out of the air and make it real. Write it out in great detail without any concern about how you will achieve it. Just be sure that it is what you want – in every detail.   Then begin to think about them all the time. (Brian Tracy)

Write us and let us know your success Stories. For more information, please contact the Special Markets Department at the Big Book Box Books Group, 4613 Lanier drive, 4th Floor, Savannah, Ga 31405,or call (912) 224-7502, or e-mail brian@10shop.com.

Table of Content   **Pages**

1. How to start a garage sales business.

Decide if you have the right personality to run a garage sale business. If you regularly hit the garage sale trail, this is the right business for you. However, you'll also need a few other skills to make your garage sale business a success. The key to running a successful business is to be well-organized, generally enjoy meeting new people, and be able to follow through and meet deadlines. Most garage sales occur on Fridays, Saturdays, and Sundays so be prepared to give up your weekend free time in order to conduct your business.

Are you ready to move forward with your garage sale business? Now it's time to form a plan. Decide if you will work alone or have a partner. Research the start-up costs involved in starting a garage sale business. Decide if you have the cash required to start the business or if you will need to find funding. Figure out how you will advertise your new business.

Once your plan is outlined, it's time to do some research. You probably already have experience in garage sales but if you're new to the idea then check out a few in your area. Talk to the people running the sale to get ideas on general organization, pricing, and set-up. Know that some of your clients will have antiques or vintage items to sell. You will need a basic education on pricing for these items in addition to knowledge on pricing less valuable items such as clothing or books. The local library or bookstore will likely have books written by experts in the field.

Start advertising. Spread the word through friends and family; keep a supply of business cards with you to hand out when the opportunity presents itself. Post an ad in the local classifieds or use free online advertising sites. Make sure that the details of your business are clear. Let potential clients know that their involvement can be minimal and completely up to them. Most likely if the client knows his or her time and involvement is minimal, the better chance you'll have of securing a contract.

Obtain necessary materials. You'll need signs to post near the sale location, a cash box, and pricing supplies. Make sure to have a supply of bags for buyers and spare extension cords to test electrical items. A basic home office for tracking clients and expenses is a good idea too.

Get to work. Start out organizing sales for friends and family then build from there. Before agreeing to run a sale, decide on your commission and draw up a contract with your client. It should list all the tasks you will be handling as well as the client's level of involvement. Depending on the amount of items to sell, you'll want to start organizing the sale a few days before the actual sale. Sort and price all the items. Pack the items in easy to carry boxes. Prior to the start of the sale, set out tables and put the sale items in an easy to reach spot such as the garage or a shed. Arrive early on sale day and organize the sale items in an attractive manner to appeal to your customers.

When the sale is over, pack up all the unsold items. Donate the items to charity or return to the client based on your agreement. Pay the client and make sure there are no lingering issues. Encourage them to let others know about your business and start preparing for your next sale.

There's just too much clutter in here!" "My house is a mess." "We need space for that brand new leather sofa." Lines we often say when we just have too much junk to handle.

Well, there is a solution and you can de-clog your house and be in business at the same time. It's time for a rummage sale also known to others as a garage sale!

It's a golden opportunity for you to get rid of the things you don't want to make room for things that you do want and also make some money on the side. It this idea tickles you, here are some suggestions to get you started.

First things first, get organized. Make a checklist of the items you want to get rid off, items that are actually still sellable and of use to others. This list will also serve as your inventory list. No under wears, bras and old socks, please. It's just to embarrassing to handle. With that out of the way, almost anything is good for a garage sale. What items can you put on this list? Items like old toys, baby cloths, old books, used clothes, caps, and maybe an old set of golf clubs. You are free to include baseball cards, stamp collections, and framed cross stitches, if you have them. The list goes on. Organize your inventory in boxes so buyers can find them easily. Sort them into categories. By the way, you may also want to pre-wash the clothes first before piling them up for sale. I also suggest you place price tags on your items so as to make purchasing easier for your buyers. Keep your prices reasonable. Remember people are looking for bargains and you want to get rid of your junk anyway. Have ample change ready as well.

Also be ready with bags or baskets your customers can use while shopping. According to experts, grocery buyers psychologically want to see their carts full because it makes them feel complete and not lacking. So use the same rational, provide them with big baskets to fill as well. You may also want to package items which you don't think will sell with stuff that are hot. This way you get to clear unwanted items as well.

Have cold drinks like soda or home made lemonade for sale too on your garage selling times. You know how buyers get all tired and thirsty as the search for a bargain. Who knows, this extra mile effort may actually make you an extra buck. Here's another tip. Have your breakables into places where they are least likely to break but where customers can see and touch them. You might also want to have an electric outlet ready so your customers can test try electrical appliances for sale.

Why not make it a family activity? You may include your kids in this project by allowing them to help out and participate. Have them help you stock, organize, label and teach them some selling lines too! Customers find that cute when seven year olds try to sell. However, do reward them for their efforts.

After organizing your garage items, now is the time to think about your date to start. I would suggest you open on a Wednesday which is mid week up until Saturday. Open late and close late on these days. You want to attract both the non-working and the working that come out of their offices after five.

Make your date of opening successful by using post ads and by placing neon bright posters that hurt the eye. Use balloons and place arrows to make it easier for your buyers to find your garage sale. Try to space your opening date 4-5 weeks ahead so people can buzz about it. Avoid opening on holidays but why not capitalize on the season, be creative!

During the garage sale itself make sure you make an effort to meet people and create relationships. Have fun selling! As an extra gesture, you may want to hand out thank you cards with your number printed at the back for every purchase your customers make but don't forget to ask for their numbers too. You can use this information later for future garage sales you might want to do. Enjoy the process and make a follow-up inventory after the day to track down your profits.

A garage sale is a great way to make extra money and help kick start your savings. All too often we over spend, finding ourselves in debt and with too much clutter. Holding a garage sale is the easiest way to remove these items from your life and recover some money in doing so.

If you no longer need or use an item; you should sell it. Having an item simply sit in a cupboard or collect dust has a two pronged negative impact; it costs you money to store and the money tied up in the item would be better placed on your credit card debt, mortgage or ideally your savings account.

2. Here is how to run a garage sale that makes money, declutters your house and converts junk into cash.

The best day of the week to hold a garage sale

The day you choose for your garage sale has the ability to make, break or explode the success of your garage sale.

So what day is best for holding a garage sale?

It is wise to note that in order to make money at your garage sale, you are going to need plenty of customers. To get plenty of customers, you are going to need to align your sale day to a day and month that is conducive to getting foot traffic into your driveway.

For this reason it is wise to not only consider the day of the week you hold your garage sale, but the time of year as well.

Saturday and Sundays are ideal days in general; this is because people work during the week and is the only two days they have 'free'. You will alienate a huge proportion of your would-be customers if you were to have a sale on a weekday.

Long weekends and public holidays can also be good; while many people go away, many people are left relaxing at home, often with nothing to do meaning more people attending your garage sale.

Warmer months of the year are also best; people tend to walk more, wander more and want to buy more when the weather is better. It also limits your chances of rain or bad weather on the day.

The best time of day to hold a garage sale

The best time of day to run a garage sale is to kick off early (around 9am) and run until 3-4pm. Most people are out and about around 12 or 1pm so that is when you will see the most foot traffic to your garage sale. The reason you should go from 9am is that is likely the time that shop owners and dealers will be out and about looking for garage sales.

3. Advertising and promoting your garage sale

In the movie 'Field of dreams' with Kevin Costner, the famous quote goes 'build it and they will come' – this does not apply here let me assure you.

To run a successful garage sale you will need to promote the hell out of it. If you don't, no one will know about it. Simple.

So what is the best way to promote and advertise a garage sale?

Make highly visible signs

You will need to create signs that are easy to read and descriptive. Your goal is to surround a 2-3 km radius of your property with signs pointing back to your address. Be careful not to make signs with small print or non-memorable details. All you need to list is the address, some prized items for sale and simple instructions like 'next left' or '30 seconds away'.

You can put signs up the week prior to build momentum if you wish, however on sale day you should replace your general marketing signs with specific location and time signs of your garage sale.

Remember, your signs need to be visible to people driving by in cars. Big, bold and clear is the goal.

You should also consider posting signs at your local shops, an array of telegraph poles, roundabouts and near local school pick-up areas. Basically you want to promote your garage sale to high traffic local areas.

Promoting your garage sale through the local newspaper

A great way to build momentum for your sale is to advertise your garage sale in your local newspaper.

It's surprising how popular these papers are for classified and real estate.

Be sure to list any big ticket or popular items in your ad; antiques and furniture do particularly well I have found.

You can also advertise your garage sale in larger newspapers like the Sydney Morning Herald but this comes with increased cost. I have done this once before and got a solid turn out; the big newspapers attract antique dealers and people who run stores.

Post your garage sale on GumTree

GumTree.com.au is a great free classifieds site. It has the potential to advertise your garage sale, free of charge, to thousands of locals. Take 15 minutes and list your garage sale and take the time to post some photos and directions.

Get your neighbours involved also

See if your neighbours would like to hold a garage sale on the same day. Inform them of all the tips and tricks to run a successful garage sale and essentially you are doubling your marketing footprint without any extra work.

Leverage council swap days for free promotion

Most councils have annual swap days or second hand sale days. If you can, align your garage sale to one of these events as you will find many people wandering the streets looking at other items.

4. Items that sell well at garage sales

Your sole goal when holding a garage sale is to make money and declutter your house. The trick is to find household items that you no longer need, or would prefer to sell, that people are going to want. If people want them, they will pay for them.

Be realistic and remember that while 'one mans trash is another mans treasure' there are limits to this saying. Don't go selling ridiculous items that no one wants; it cheapens your garage sale and loads it with junk.

Instead, focus on items that are going to sell really well. From personal experience I have found the following will often sell really well at a garage sale.

Before you read on, we have also compiled a great list of things to sell for extra money that could apply to your garage sale also.

Power tools

Items like old mowers, whipper snippers, power drills and hedge trimmers are sought after items that always sell fast.

Just about any power tool or gardening device will sell, and sell well.

These are items that sell for a premium in most hardware stores so don't be affraid to put a decent price on your tools. A lawn mower for instance will likely cost over $500 to buy brand new; a second hand one you could easily sell for $50 to $100 and the prospective buyer would still be getting a great deal (as you can repair a lawn mower for next to nothing).

Childrens toys, clothes and other household items

Items like high chairs, play mats, play pens, nappy bags, Fisher Price toys and other baby items will always sell quickly.

Having a newborn is expensive and many people search garage sales for cheap kids toys and items; a great way to save money and not pay retail price.

Most mums fail to let go of baby items, holding them for many years in case another child comes along or in the case of my mother in law, she simply holds many memories with each item and cannot bare to let it go.

The truth is however, baby items that sit in a cupboard for five years are not going to help you. Sell them now, make the money now and if you really are unsure if you are going to have another child; simply invest the earnings from those items into a term deposit or similar for safe keeping.

Brand new items that are still in a box

We all have weird presents given to us that simply stay in the box they came in. These are great items to sell at a garage sale as they will appear brand new, have a very low price and someone can easily re-gift them and snag a bargain in doing so.

Look for old Christmas presents, birthday presents or gifts that were given to you as souvenirs when people travelled (you know, the horrible beach towel from Scotland that has a kilt printed on it? Yeah sell it).

Antiques sell really well at garage sales

Antiques and retro items are always popular at garage sales. People love to buy a piece of history or something that could be a talking point in their house.

Items that sell well include antique phones from the 70's, jugs and cutlery, vintage jewelry and old Australiana items that could be hung up in the yard.

Furniture is always wanted at a garage sale

Desks, chairs, tables, benches and couches are always super popular for garage sales. You often get second hand furniture shops scanning the newspaper for upcoming garage sales and if you have taken out a newspaper ad as mentioned above, you are certain to have them come by.

Old furniture is often made of hardwood and can be rejuvenated to look amazing. Couple this with the fact that modern furniture is often made cheaply and of poor materials, the older furniture is becoming more and more sought after.

We once had a garage sale and listed multiple hardwood desks for sale; we had furniture dealers arrive 2 hours before the garage sale started trying to make an offer before the public saw the items. That is how much people love furniture at garage sales!

White goods (fridges, washing machines, dryers and more)

Household appliances like fridges and washing machines always sell well at a garage sale. Uni students, share houses and renters are always looking to save money on these items and garage sales are the best bet for them.

Advertise the white goods in all of your garage sale marketing tactics and don't bring them items to the front of your garage. Simply take a photo of them and print them onto A4 paper for people to see; if they are genuinely interested you can take them to the item.

Remember, it's up to them to pick up the item as you don't want to be offering a delivery service (though if you do, charge an extra $25 for home delivery).

Pricing your garage sale items to sell

To ensure your items sell you need to:

Use big stickers that are colour coded and clearly priced. The bigger the price tag the more likely someone is to pick up the item for further inspection. Set some consistant pricing via the colour coding; blue is $2, red is $5 and so on.

Be realistic with your pricing; if you think something is worth $5, price it at $3. You want to sell your items not debate their value with passers-by.

When you have crowds of people there; tell them out loud that everything must go and to make an offer fast.

At the end of the garage sale time slot; offer all items for $2 or something trivial as odds are they will be going in the bin if they don't sell.

Displaying your items logically to make it easier for people to buy

Group like items onto similar tables.

Use trestle tables and white table clothes to make items stand out.

Bundle items for sale; don't sell one book for 50 cents, sell 10 for $5.00.

Make sure your items are tidy and clean; showcase them like you would in a store.

Display your high value or 'sellable' items at the front; if people love power tools, promote your power tools with the best real estate at your garage sale.

5. Protecting your items from theft at a garage sale

Be careful when holding a garage sale as quite often I have seen things go missing. It saddens me that people would actually steal from someone trying to sell their belongings but the fact remains that it does happen.

Put valuable items on a table that is hard to reach or re□uires you to manage (e.g. handing the item to people who wish to look).

Also be sure to lock your house up nice and tight; I have heard stories of people wandering into a house while the owner holds the garage sale out the front.

The best garage sale tip I can give is to setup tables in such a way as to block access to your house (hopefully) and limit the ability to lose high value items when you aren't looking.

How to handle the admin of a garage sale

Manage your inventory and prices wisely. Prior to the garage sale, list all of the items you are selling and note their price. This will act as a □uick reference guide on the day if you lose your stickers or wish to cross items off as you sell them.

Get a bumbag. Fill it with about $20 worth of every coin (for change) and be sure to have lots of smaller notes (5's, 10's, 20's). Make sure you separate coins with coin bags you get from the bank to make it easier to find change.

Print off some receipt templates. Some people will ask for a receipt with their purchase; use a template to write the item name, item price and date.

Get someone to help you on the day. To hold a successful garage sale, you will likely need three people. A person to man the tables, a person to show people bigger items and another admin support person to help with receipts, change and other tasks.

Want to make extra money at a garage sale? Consider holding a sausage sizzle on your front lawn for $1 or $2 a pop with $1.50 cans of drink. Only do this if you are confident that you will get a lot of foot traffic in your area.

Maximise your selling space. Use your driveway, carport and entire front lawn if you can. Try not to make the event feel too crowded.

Be proactive in your selling. Talk with buyers, tell them about the item they are touching, sell its condition and multiple uses. If you really want to, you can offer them a discount immediately to lure them into a deal.

Cross sell items at your garage sale. If someone buys the lawnmower, they should also buy the jerry can full of petrol as well. Pair up items and try and offload multiple items per transaction.

Haggling and bargaining at a garage sale

Garage sales are notorious for attracting bargain hunters. People craving a good deal. In fact, most people I have seen at a garage sale appear to get a thrill from trying to haggle.

The trick to managing people who are wanting to haggle is to make them feel like they are getting a good deal. If they offer a low price, tell them you are happy to meet them halfway between that price and your original asking price. It's a fair and reasonable request for both sides.

Remember, stay strong on big ticket items that are popular or genuinely worth the money. If the item is a small keepsake or piece of junk; accept any offers as it's better than putting it in the bin.

6. How to Have a Successful Garage Sale – Tips for Pricing Items

Few things make me happier than turning my unwanted clutter into cash. There are several ways to do this, including selling on Craigslist, setting up auctions on eBay, and utilizing newspaper classifieds. However, I've found that a good old-fashioned garage sale often works best, especially when you have a lot of small things to sell.

Having a garage sale takes work and can be extremely frustrating if you don't know what you're doing. To avoid any headaches and to streamline the process, follow a plan from beginning to end. A well-planned garage sale often means a more successful one, which means more money in your pocket at the end of the day.

Planning Your Garage Sale

1. Pick a Date

The first step is to choose dates and times for your garage sale. Most people go with Friday and Saturday mornings, but you can add Thursday or Sunday to a multi-day sale if your schedule allows. You'll get a larger crowd if you start early because people won't have to interrupt their day to attend your sale, and it's likely to be cooler out which is an important consideration especially in the heat of summer. I typically run my garage sales Friday and Saturday from 6 a.m. to noon.

Pro Tip: If possible, hold your garage sale when the weather is moderate. Skipping out on the sweltering August heat and waiting for the end of September will give you a better shot at having a successful sale. You'll get the most customers in the late spring or early fall.

2. Gather Your Goods

Garage sales offer a great way to declutter and downsize your house. Grab a box and go through every room. Pick up anything you don't want or haven't used in months and toss it in. Don't forget closets, attics, basements, and garages as these are usually treasure troves for garage sale finds. Don't underestimate the value of what you find either; people will buy anything from old CDs to unwanted bottles of perfume. After all, the worst case scenario is that something doesn't sell.

Pro Tip: Have any old power strips, cell phone chargers, or USB cables you're not using? Throw them in a separate shoe box to sell at the garage sale. It doesn't matter if you're not sure what that charger even worked for; someone may buy it.

3. Check on Permits

Many cities now require that you have a permit to run a garage sale. Check with a clerk at your city or town hall to find out if you need one. Don't try to run a garage sale without it or you may end up getting shut down and fined.

Pro Tip: Some cities allow you to apply for permits online. Check your town hall website and look under the "permits" or "civic responsibilities" section to see where you can apply.

1. Create a Newspaper Ad

If you want to drive major traffic to your garage sale, fork up the money to pay for an ad in your local newspaper. But before you write your ad, find out how much space you get for the price you're willing to pay. If you go over, you'll end up paying per word, which can get very expensive fast. Keep your ad short and pointed, and list your biggest ticket items first. The most popular garage sale items include furniture, kids' toys, and collectibles. Don't forget to include your address as well as the dates and times your sale will run.

Pro Tip: Consider advertising in your local paper as well as the major daily newspaper in your area. Most local papers charge $15 or less for ad space, and every home in the area gets a free copy, which means more potential customers for you.

2. Advertise Online

There are dozens of websites where you can advertise your garage sale for free. Post an ad on as many as you want, but aim for at least three. For example, I use:

Garage Sale Source

You'll have more wiggle room in the text of your online ad since most websites give you a generous word count. Feel free to describe your items in detail, but avoid sounding like a marketing executive. Simply tell people what you have and when you'll have it, and let their own imaginations work out how wonderful it is. Also, don't post your ad too early. If you're holding your garage sale on Friday, it should go up Wednesday night or Thursday afternoon.

It's also a great idea to utilize free social media marketing sites to get the word out in your local area.

Pro Tip: Write your ad in a word processing program and simply copy and paste it to each listing website site. This will save you the hassle of retyping it over and over again.

3. Make Yard Sale Signs

Check the laws in your area before making garage sale signs as some places have banned them. A clerk at your local police station can tell what you can and can't do. If you are allowed to make signs, I've found that brightly colored poster board and a Sharpie is all you really need. Make sure your sign says "Garage Sale" large enough for people to see as they drive by. Include your address or an arrow pointing towards your house.

Pro Tip: Wood paint stirrers make great posts for sticking garage sale signs in the ground. You can get the stirrers free from most home improvement stores.

garage sales newspaper

Prepping for the Sale

1. Get Supplies

Make sure you have everything you need at least a day before the garage sale starts. You'll need chairs to sit on, a table or other flat surface to take payments and provide change, and plenty of areas to display your goods. Don't waste money on renting or buying tables. You can find or make enough surfaces to suit your needs.

For example, I gather up all of the card tables and patio furniture I can find for placing breakable items on. For smaller, non-breakable items, I put a board over two milk crates. For clothes, you can use a garment rack or hang them on hangers off the top of your garage door.

Tip: Keep tables with breakables off to the side of your sale or against a fence. Unattended kids love to run underneath tables, so the more centrally located they are, the higher risk you run of the table being knocked over.

2. Don't Forget the Change

Odds are, you'll have to make $19.95 in change for your first customer. Make sure you have fives, ones, and at least twenty dollars in ⬚uarters. You can get them from your bank, but you'll have to go inside a branch to do it.

Tip: Ask the bank for a reusable cash envelope. Many branches are happy to give you one. You can use the envelope to run extra money back into the house throughout the garage sale so you won't have tons of cash lying around outside.

3. Sort Your Items

Sort before your price. It's the easiest way to keep your garage sale organized and make it easy on potential buyers. Dedicate a room in your house to garage sale planning and divide all of your items by category, such as clothes, books, home goods, and kids' toys.

Tip: If you have a lot of clothes, divide them by men's, women's, and children's. Most people are looking for something specific and will appreciate the organization.

4. Price Your Items

It's best if you price your items individually rather than just group them into boxes with one price sign. As the garage sale progresses, people will get the boxes mixed up and you'll have a hard time keeping it organized. To price items, I just use a roll of manila tape and a Sharpie, which is a lot cheaper than going out and buying fancy price tags.

Tip: Don't increase your prices on the assumption that everyone likes to haggle. While many people do enjoy a good verbal match, some will just walk away if they think items are priced too high.

5. Organize and Arrange Your Sale

Arrange your tables and put all the clothes on hangers the night before the garage sale. No matter what you tell yourself, you won't have enough time to do it in the morning. I arrange everything the night before and store it in the garage for safekeeping. Map out where everything will be placed to make the morning setup as easy as possible and to keep it in a logical and organized fashion for customers.

Tip: If you can't put everything in the garage the night before, group similar items into laundry baskets and boxes. You will save time in the morning if you only have to pull items out of boxes that don't require further separation.

Garage sale for people

Throwing Your Garage Sale

1. Get Ready

Give yourself at least an hour before the garage sale starts to set everything out and put up signs. Make sure you have your change in a safe place, and find a comfortable, shaded area to sit.

Tip: If your garage sale is hard to spot from the street, place a yard sale sign in front of your house so people know where to stop.

2. Work the Crowd

In an ideal world, a garage sale would work like Target. People would come in, grab what they wanted, pay, and leave. Unfortunately, people see garage sales as a sort of interactive shopping experience. They're going to ask questions, they're going to haggle, and they're going to pick up everything, especially if it's breakable. You'll do better if you don't act pushy. Just stay seated, shout out a friendly hello when people walk up, and let the customers come to you.

Keep in mind that you don't have to haggle right away. Don't let your couch go for five dollars with the first customer. Odds are that someone else will come along willing to pay your asking price. Start haggling like crazy using effective negotiation strategies on the last day, or in the afternoons after the morning rush.

Tip: Position your chair so that you can easily spot people walking up and make sure you greet everyone. Saying a quick hello makes shoppers more comfortable about standing in your driveway.

3. Deal with Leftovers

You're going to have leftover stuff. You can just put it all on the curb with a free sign, but that won't get you any more money. Instead, consider taking the leftovers to a Goodwill store and save on your taxes. Make an itemized list of everything you have with its original value. Once you drop it at a donation center, ask for a receipt. File this away to use for a tax deduction for charitable donations on your income taxes.

Tip: If you have large items left over, like a couch or a TV set, consider selling them on Craigslist. Craigslist surfers love to buy big-ticket items and you'll make more money than you would donating them and using the tax deduction.

Final Word

Garage sales are a lot of work, especially if you're not used to holding them. You'll probably spend several hours organizing and pricing items, writing ads, and getting your supplies. But after it's over, you'll hopefully have a wad of cash instead of piles of stuff you don't want, which makes it all worthwhile.

Have you ever thrown a garage sale? What are some of the methods that have worked best for you?

A Garage Sale Business Can Be Profitable!

7. Organizing Garage Sales Can be Profitable!

Need extra money? Especially during the recession, organizing a garage sale business, at your home on weekends, especially during the summer, can be a profitable, low risk way to start a home-based business, and get extra income. Besides selling your unwanted, excess, or unused items (but that's a good place to start), you can buy wholesale merchandise from wholesale companies that cater in part to people selling at garage sales.

The great American garage sale, also known as a yard sale, rummage sale, moving sale, or block sale, is quickly becoming more than a place to find or get rid of old, unused, household junk. Because of the recession and to save money, many smart shoppers are shunning department stores, shopping malls, and the Internet, and turning to garage sales to meet most of their material needs.

On any summer weekend, take a drive through any American suburb, residential neighborhood, for example, around Portland Oregon, San Francisco, New York, Miami, and you will see what I mean. People are loving garage sales all over America. There, you can find anything from household items for 50 cents each to appliances like a television and refrigerator, other household furnishings, such as sofas, dinning room table sets, even valuable collectables, at a small fraction of the price found shopping downtown.

Setting Up the Sale

Use the driveway as the main selling area, then the front porch, lawn, or other parts of the front yard as needed. Use tables as much as possible to display your items. Keep different types of merchandise clean and separate from each other. For example, keep clothing like shirts, jackets together, and clothing should be on cloths hangers and racks. Glass wear, pottery, etc. should all be together, and so on. Maintain clear traffic isles. The better your sale looks and the more you have out, the more people will stop to see what you have!

Garage Sale Pricing

Most people come to this type of sale in search of bargains. So give them bargains! It depends on what you are selling, but for larger articles, for example: a three-man dome tent, good condition, try selling for 1/4 the original value. Use the same pricing for such things as a washer or dryer, dinning room table set. Be careful! Don't sell something, then later regret selling it. Sell only merchandise you won't mind selling, stuff that you just want to move out. Most used shirts sell for $1-2; same with old pants (except jeans, sell for more depending on its condition); glass wear 50¢ to $1.

If you try purchasing from wholesale companies with the intention of reselling it at your sale, fine. But make sure you can sell it at a price that will give you a good profit. It takes some experience. Small flags for example, American flags, Mexican flags, other flags too, sell pretty well during certain times of the year or on holidays. Just make sure there is a good market for your purchases and shop only from a genuine wholesale supplier. You can go to my website (see link below) for a free list of genuine wholesale companies.

Put Out Lots of Signs

Place informative signs at strategic locations and intersections to direct people to your sale. A small, saw horse type sign, which you can easily make yourself, stands nicely and you can fold it up to be used another day. Or, you can use signs with wooden rods attached to push or pound into the dirt or a lawn. The more difficult it is to find your home, the more signs you will need to put out. Make them bold and colorful to attract more attention.

Advertise

You can place free Internet classified advertising listings on Craigslist.org and many local news publications allow free classified ads as well. Of course, the more signs, ads, fliers you put out there, the more traffic you will draw and the more $$$ of profits you will make! So, as in any small business enterprise, promote! promote!

Comments